Zoom In on

Native American Leaders

Crazy Horse

Jennifer Strand

abdopublishing.com

Published by Abdo Zoom™, PO Box 398166, Minneapolis, Minnesota 55439. Copyright © 2018 by
Abdo Consulting Group, Inc. International copyrights reserved in all countries. No part of this book may be
reproduced in any form without written permission from the publisher. Abdo Zoom™ is a trademark and logo
of Abdo Consulting Group, Inc.

Printed in the United States of America, North Mankato, Minnesota
052017
092017

**THIS BOOK CONTAINS
RECYCLED MATERIALS**

Cover Photo: Bettmann/Getty Images
Interior Photos: Bettmann/Getty Images, 1, 19; Robert Cicchetti/iStockphoto, 4–5; iStockphoto, 5, 16–17; Robert
Cicchetti/Shutterstock Images, 6–7; Karen Parker/iStockphoto, 8; Everett Historical/Shutterstock Images, 9, 12, 13,
15; Ann Ronan Pictures/Print Collector/Hulton Archive/Getty Images, 10; Z. R. F. Photo/iStockphoto, 11; Palmquist
& Jurgens/Library of Congress, 14; Interim Archives/Archive Photos/Getty Images, 17; River North Photography/
iStockphoto, 18

Editor: Emily Temple
Series Designer: Madeline Berger
Art Direction: Dorothy Toth

Publisher's Cataloging-in-Publication Data
Names: Strand, Jennifer, author.
Title: Crazy Horse / by Jennifer Strand.
Description: Minneapolis, MN : Abdo Zoom, 2018. | Series: Native American
    leaders | Includes bibliographical references and index.
Identifiers: LCCN 2017931230 | ISBN 9781532120237 (lib. bdg.) |
    ISBN 9781614797340 (ebook) | 9781614797906 (Read-to-me ebook)
Subjects: LCSH: Crazy Horse, approximately 1842-1877--Juvenile literature. |
    Oglala Indians--Kings and rulers--Biography--Juvenile literature.
Classification: DDC 978.004/9752/092 [B]--dc23
LC record available at http://lccn.loc.gov/2017931230

Table of Contents

Introduction

Crazy Horse was a Native American warrior. He worked hard to protect his **tribe**.

He tried to keep US settlers
from taking his tribe's land.

Early Life

Crazy Horse was
born around 1842.

He lived on the Great Plains. He was part of the Oglala Lakota tribe.

Crazy Horse learned how to ride horses. He also learned to hunt.

When he was a teenager
he became a warrior.

Leader

Crazy Horse was known
for being brave.

His people controlled a lot of land.

Gold was found on Lakota land. The settlers wanted the gold.

The US government tried to make the tribe move to **reservations**.

In 1876 the US army attacked. Crazy Horse joined **Chief** Sitting Bull.

14

They worked together to fight US soldiers. The Native Americans won. It was a big victory.

15

After the battle, Crazy Horse led his people into the hills. They kept their way of life for a while.

But soon they ran out of food.
They had to **surrender**.

Legacy

Crazy Horse died on
September 5, 1877.

He is remembered as a great leader.

Crazy Horse

Born: around 1842, the exact date is not known

Birthplace: near modern-day Rapid City, South Dakota

Known For: Crazy Horse was a famous Lakota warrior. A giant sculpture is being built in his honor in South Dakota.

Died: September 5, 1877

Key Dates

1842: Crazy Horse is born around this time. No one knows the exact date.

1874: Gold is found on Lakota land. Settlers try to take the land from the Lakota tribe.

1875: The US government says the Lakota tribe must move to reservations.

1876: Crazy Horse and Sitting Bull lead a battle against the US Army.

1877: Crazy Horse and his tribe surrender. He dies on September 5.

Glossary

chief - the leader of a group of people.

reservation - an area of land in the United States that is set aside for Native Americans to live.

settler - a person who goes to live in a new place.

surrender - when a group agrees to stop fighting or hiding because they know they will not win.

tribe - a group of people who share the same culture and beliefs.

Booklinks

For more information on **Crazy Horse**, please visit abdobooklinks.com

Zoom In on Biographies!

Learn even more with the Abdo Zoom Biographies database. Check out **abdozoom.com** for more information.

Index